Grammar, Spelling & Vocabulary

Activity Book

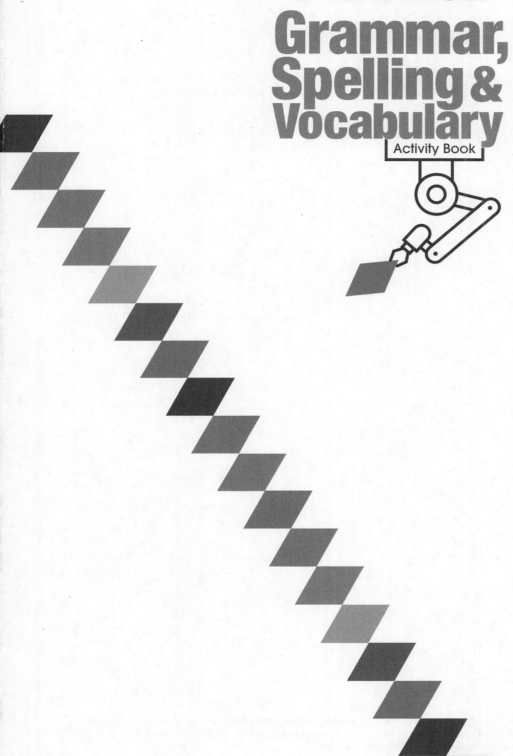

Benchmark Education Company
145 Huguenot Street • New Rochelle, NY 10801

Project Editors: Lisa Yelsey and Rose Birnbaum   Creative Director: Laurie Berger   Art Director: Glenn Davis

Printed in Guangzhou, China. 4401/1119/CA21901994

ISBN: 978-1-5125-7836-2

Table of Contents

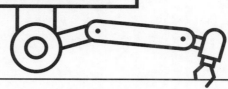

Grammar

Concrete and Abstract Nouns

Concrete nouns name things you can see, hear, smell, touch, or taste. **Auditorium**, **sunset**, **cupcake**, and **music** are examples of concrete nouns.

Abstract nouns name things that you cannot experience with one of your five senses. **Truth**, **honesty**, **luck**, **brilliance**, and **delight** are examples of abstract nouns.

faith	mountains	disappointment	candidates
confidence	kindness	sunlight	sister

Determine whether each noun in the box is concrete or abstract. Write the words in the correct chart below.

Concrete Nouns	Abstract Nouns

Write a noun from one of the lists above to complete each sentence.

1. It was a huge _____ to Marisa to be sick on field day.

2. Thank you for your _____ toward our new students.

3. My _____ is two years older than I am.

4. The _____ look magnificent in the morning light.

Name _____ Date _____

Concrete and Abstract Nouns

Concrete nouns name things you can see, hear, smell, touch, or taste. **Piano**, **icicle**, **volunteers**, and **burrito** are examples of concrete nouns.

Abstract nouns name things that you cannot experience with one of your five senses. **Respect**, **friendship**, **childhood**, and **justice** are examples of abstract nouns.

Circle whether the underlined noun in each sentence is concrete or abstract.

1. The <u>history</u> of my family began in Vietnam.

   concrete   abstract

2. <u>Mrs. Rivera</u> shows compassion to all her students.

   concrete   abstract

3. I have a lot of <u>respect</u> for our environment.

   concrete   abstract

4. The <u>office</u> of president can be held for up to eight years.

   concrete   abstract

5. I do not want to be sent to the principal's <u>office</u>.

   concrete   abstract

For each sentence, write the abstract noun in the sentence on the line.

6. My father takes pride in his cooking. _____

7. Honesty is important to me. _____

8. We have the freedom to choose a new class song. _____

Regular Verbs and Verb Tenses

A verb is a word that shows action.

Present tense verbs tell about something that is happening now.

Present: I **help** my family with household chores.

Past tense verbs tell about something that has already happened.

Past: Yesterday, I **helped** my brother clean his room.

Future tense verbs tell about something that will happen at a later time.

Future: I **will help** my sister set the table tonight.

Choose the correct tense of the verb _board, release,_ or _welcome_ to complete each sentence. Write the verb on the line.

board	boarded	will board
release	released	will release
welcome	welcomed	will welcome

1. We _____ the plane over an hour ago.

2. The band _____ their first song next year.

3. Please _____ José to our class.

4. My neighbors _____ a new baby in a few months.

5. I _____ the dogs from their leashes when we got home.

6. We _____ the bus at the next corner.

Grammar, Spelling & Vocabulary Activity Book • © Benchmark Education Company, LLC   G3 U1 W2 BLM1

Regular Verbs and Verb Tenses

Regular past tense verbs end in **-ed**, but the rules on how this ending to the verb differ, depending on how the verb is spelled.

For most regular verbs, add **-ed**.	spill + **ed**	spilled
If a verb ends in **-e**, just add **-d**.	advanc**e** + **d**	advanced
If a verb ends in a vowel and a single consonant, double the consonant and add **-ed**.	st**op** + **p** + **ed**	stopped
If a verb ends in a consonant and **-y**, change the **-y** to **-i** and add **-ed**.	mar**ry** mar**ri** + **ed**	married

Write the past tense form of the verb in ( ) on the line.

1. Yesterday, Tomas and I (watch)_____ a great movie.

2. The baby (cry) _____ because she was hungry.

3. Were you (invite)_____ to your uncle's wedding?

4. I (spot) _____ my friends in the crowd.

5. Thomas Edison (invent) _____ many useful things.

6. It was such a warm day that we (decide) _____ to walk home.

7. I am not (allow) _____ to go to the city by myself.

Subject-Verb Agreement

The subject of a sentence tells whom or what the sentence is about. The verb is an action word that tells what the subject is or does. The subject and the verb in a sentence must agree in number and person. Most singular verbs end in **-s**. Removing the final **-s** makes the verbs plural.

Those **boys play** basketball.

That **girl plays** soccer.

Determine whether the subject in each sentence is singular or plural. Circle the correct form of the verb. Then write the verb on the line.

1. Trevor _____ the plates on the top shelf.

   place   places

2. Marissa _____ the piano very well.

   play   plays

3. My friends _____ in the chorus.

   sing   sings

4. Ray _____ many history books.

   read   reads

5. The roses _____ so sweet!

   smell   smells

Capitalize Titles

Words We Capitalize in a Book or Movie Title	Words We Usually Don't Capitalize in a Book or Movie Title*
• the first word • the last word • nouns • pronouns • verbs • adjectives • adverbs	• the articles **a, and,** and **the** in the middle of the title • conjunctions such as **and, but, or,** and **nor** in the middle of the title • short prepositions such as **of, for, to, on, in, as,** and **by** in the middle of the title

* If it is the first word in a subtitle (the first word after a colon), capitalize it.

Use the rules above to rewrite each title correctly on the line.

1. beauty And The beast

_____

2. star wars: the force awakens

_____

3. james and the giant Peach

_____

4. stink: the incredible shrinking kid

_____

5. encyclopedia brown, boy detective

_____

6. the wizard of oz

_____

Adjectives and Adverbs

Adjectives describe, or tell more about, nouns and pronouns.

Yuri is a **thoughtful** friend. He sent Rita a **dozen red** roses.

Adverbs describe or tell more about verbs, adjectives, and other adverbs.

The truck drove **very slowly** up the street. Then it stopped **completely**.

Circle whether the word in dark type is an adjective or an adverb. Then underline the word it describes.

1. The tortoise and the hare had an **important** race.

    adjective   adverb

2. The hare sprinted **away** from the starting point.

    adjective   adverb

3. The **enormous** tortoise lumbered down the road.

    adjective   adverb

4. The hare **mistakenly** believed he would win.

    adjective   adverb

5. He decided to take a **brief** nap along the way.

    adjective   adverb

Punctuate Dialogue

Dialogue is a conversation between two or more characters in a story. Quotation marks show the exact words a character says. A writer uses commas to separate the names of the speakers from the words they say. Look at the examples below.

Monique said, "We must all have positive attitudes."
"We must all have positive attitudes," said Monique.

Read each sentence. Then rewrite it using the correct punctuation.

1. Maria said I will start my homework after dinner.

_____

2. I hope you won't stay up too late said Dad.

_____

3. I have a lot of homework replied Maria. I'll start now.

_____

4. Mom said I'll call you when dinner is ready.

_____

5. Thanks, Mom said Maria.

_____

6. Mom called Maria! Don't forget your books!

_____

Coordinating Conjunctions to Form Compound Sentences

A coordinating conjunction and comma connect two simple sentences to form a compound sentence. The words **and**, **or**, **but**, and **so** are coordinating conjunctions.

Simple sentences: I like spinach. I don't like kale.
Compound sentence: I like spinach, **but** I don't like kale.

Rewrite the two simple sentences to form a compound sentence. Use one of the coordinating conjunctions, *and*, *or*, *but*, or *so*, and a comma.

1. It was raining hard. The baseball game was called off.

_____

2. Cedric needs new shoes. He needs a warm coat.

_____

3. I speak Spanish at home. I speak English in school.

_____

4. I might buy the book. I might get it at the library.

_____

5. Jonas was thirsty. He got a glass of water.

_____

6. I don't sing very well. I can't dance.

_____

Coordinating Conjunctions to Form Compound Sentences

The words **and**, **or**, **but**, and **so** are coordinating conjunctions. They show how the two parts of a compound sentence are related. Always place a comma before a coordinating conjunction in a compound sentence. The comma shows where one thought ends and the other begins.

It will rain today, **and** it might snow tonight. (**and** adds information)

Do you want pizza, **or** would you prefer pasta? (**or** shows a choice)

I can't go now, **but** I can go later. (**but** shows a contrast)

It might snow later, **so** I'll wear my boots. (**so** shows a result)

Write one of the following coordinating conjunctions that best shows how the parts of the sentence are related: *and, or, but,* or *so.*

1. Nina doesn't eat meat, _____ she does eat fish.

2. Josh was feverish, _____ he had a sore throat.

3. My brother likes soccer, _____ he doesn't like football.

4. I might go to the movies, _____ I might go to the concert.

5. Anna's bike had a flat tire, _____ she couldn't ride it.

6. We needed milk, _____ I went to the supermarket.

7. Mr. Raman plays football, _____ he coaches basketball, too.

8. I can walk to school, _____ I can take the bus.

Subordinating Conjunctions to Form Complex Sentences

A subordinating conjunction connects two simple sentences to form a complex sentence. Some coordinating conjunctions are **although**, **because**, **if**, **when**, **before**, and **until**.

Simple sentences: I loved the movie. It was really exciting.
Complex sentence: I loved the movie **because** it was really exciting.

Write one of the following subordinating conjunctions to complete each sentence: *although, because, if, when, before, until.*

1. Please stop at the store _____ it's out of your way.

2. Kim brushes her teeth _____ she goes to sleep.

3. My cat sits at my feet _____ we are having dinner.

4. Henry practices the piano _____ he doesn't make any mistakes.

5. We can have a picnic _____ it doesn't rain.

6. I did well on the test _____ I studied hard.

7. I go to the park _____ the weather is nice.

Subordinating Conjunctions to Form Complex Sentences

A subordinating conjunction connects two simple sentences to form a complex sentence. Examples of subordinating conjunctions are **since**, **unless**, **while**, **before**, and **after**.

We'll play soccer **unless** the field is too wet.
Our dog takes a nap **after** he runs in the park.

Rewrite the two simple sentences to form a complex sentence. Use one of the subordinating conjunctions: *since, unless, while, before,* or *after*.

1. Carla can go to bed at 9:00. She is in third grade now.

_____

2. I changed my sheets. I made my bed.

_____

3. We can go swimming. It stopped raining.

_____

4. You can't play video games. Finish your homework first.

_____

5. We will go home. The actors take their bows.

_____

6. Bruno watched TV. His brother was having his teeth cleaned.

_____

Regular Verbs and Verb Tenses

A verb is a word that shows action.

Present tense verbs tell about something that is happening now.

·Past tense verbs tell about something that has already happened.

Future tense verbs tell about something that will happen at a later time.

Circle the form of the verb that correctly completes each sentence. Write the verb, on the line.

1. When I was young, I _____.

crawl   crawled   will crawl

2. We _____ soccer later unless there is a thunderstorm.

play   played   will play

3. The team must _____ at the field on time.

arrive   arrived   will arrive

Rewrite each sentence using the past tense of the verb.

4. I will stop at my cousin's house on my way home.

_____

5. I will try to replace the flat tire on his bike.

_____

6. I will fix the tire by adding more air.

_____

Subject-Verb Agreement

The subject of a sentence is a noun that tells whom or what the sentence is about. The verb is an action word that tells what the subject is or does. The subject and the verb in a sentence must match in number (singular or plural).
Singular: Valerie loves her brothers very much.
Plural: Ben and Marco love their sister, too.

Determine whether the subject in each sentence is singular or plural. Circle the correct form of the verb. Fill in the blank in each sentence with the circled verb. Then write the complete sentence on the line.

1. Mara _____ the violin every day.
        practice   practices

_____

2. All the students _____ the bus to school.
         takes   take

_____

3. We _____ paper and plastic at home.
    recycle   recycles

_____

4. Both of my cats _____ under my bed.
      hide   hides

_____

5. My mother _____ kindergarten.
      teach   teaches

_____

Punctuate Dialogue

Dialogue is a conversation between two or more characters in a story. Quotation marks show the exact words a character says. A comma separates the speaker's introduction or tag from the words they say.

Henry said, "We should all try to get along."

"We should all try to get along," **said Henry.**

Read each sentence. Then rewrite the sentence, punctuating it correctly.

1. Matt said Let's meet at the library after school.

_____

2. I can be there by four o'clock answered Juan.

_____

3. Anna said I'm right here behind you.

_____

4. I can't believe that you didn't call me exclaimed Mark.

_____

5. Gina replied I was so busy last night that I forgot.

_____

6. I'm sorry added Gina. I won't forget again.

_____

7. The librarian said Please be quiet.

_____

Adjectives and Adverbs

Part of Speech	Examples
Adjectives describe or tell more about nouns and pronouns.	green, tall, scared, wealthy, sour, intelligent
Adverbs describe or tell more about verbs, adjectives, and other adverbs.	honestly, foolishly, kindly, usually, very, down, up

Circle the adjective in each sentence. Underline the word it describes.

1. We approached the spookiest house I have ever seen.

2. Justin walked up the crumbling steps.

3. He pushed the ancient doorbell, and the door swung open.

4. "Who's there?" asked a mysterious voice.

Circle the adverb in each sentence. Underline the word it describes.

5. Justin gasped loudly.

6. He scrambled quickly down the steps with terror on his face.

7. Justin's adventure ended badly!

Coordinating Conjunctions to Form Compound Sentences

You can combine two simple sentences with a coordinating conjunction such as **and, or, but**, and **so** to form a compound sentence. Always use a comma before a coordinating conjunction.

Simple sentences: I enjoy skiing. I like ice-skating more.

Compound sentence: I enjoy skiing, **but** I like ice-skating more.

Circle the coordinating conjunction that correctly joins the simple sentences. Write the compound sentence on the line.

1. John saw a movie last week. He went to a concert.

      and   but   or

_____

2. I called my mother. She won't worry about me.

      but   and   so

_____

3. Helena can't come over now. She can come over later.

      or   and   but

_____

4. Should I get a kitten? Should I get an older cat?

      or   so   and

_____

5. I set my alarm. I'm sure I won't oversleep.

      but   so   and

_____

Subordinating Conjunctions to Form Complex Sentences

A subordinating conjunction connects a simple sentence and a fragment to form a complex sentence. The words **although**, **because**, **when**, **unless**, **while**, and **after** are subordinating conjunctions.

I love to visit my aunt **because** she is so much fun.

I will visit her today **unless** practice runs late.

Circle the subordinating conjunction that correctly completes each complex sentence. Write the subordinating conjunction on the line.

1. I will save you a seat _____ you get there first.

   although   unless   when

2. Nina said she was sorry _____ I'm not sure she means it.

   after   although   while

3. Please report to the gym _____ you arrive.

   when   because   although

4. I don't have enough money _____ I spent it all.

   while   although   because

5. Please try to be quiet _____ the baby wakes up.

   until   because   while

6. I will put the dishes away _____ you washed them.

   before   unless   since

Possessives

Possessive nouns show that something belongs to one or more people, places, or things.

Add **'s** to a singular noun to show that something belongs to it. Example: <u>The castle that belonged to the prince</u> was made of stone. The **prince's** castle was made of stone.

Add an **'** after the final **s** in a regular plural noun to show possession. Example: <u>The castles that belonged to the princes</u> were made of stone. The **princes'** castles were made of stone.

Write the possessive form of each underlined noun.

1. the courage of the <u>firefighter</u>   the _____ courage

2. the science class of <u>Ms. Wu</u>.   _____ science class

3. the cars of your <u>brothers</u>   your _____ cars

4. the sister of my <u>father</u>.   my _____ sister

Rewrite each sentence, replacing the underlined words with a possessive phrase.

5. <u>The three puppies of my dog</u> are adorable.

_____

6. We replaced <u>the batteries in our smoke detector.</u>

_____

 Grammar, Spelling & Vocabulary Activity Book • © Benchmark Education Company, LLC

Possessives

Possessive nouns show that something belongs to one or more people, places, or things.

Add **'s** to a singular noun to show that something belongs to it—**Max's** shoes.

Add an **'** after the final **s** in a regular plural noun to show possession.

Flowers' petals.

Some nouns have irregular plural forms, such as **mice, children, people, men,** and **women**. Use **'s** to show possession with irregular plural nouns—the **women's** team.

On the line, write the possessive form of each underlined plural noun.

1. the courage of the <u>soldiers</u>   the _____ courage

2. the kids of our <u>neighbors</u>   our _____ kids

3. the pets of some <u>people</u>   some _____ pets

4. the children of your <u>aunts</u>   your _____ children

Rewrite each sentence, replacing the underlined words with a possessive phrase.

5. The <u>basketball team of the men</u> plays on Sunday.

_____

6. I brush the <u>manes of the horses.</u>

_____

Name _____ Date _____

Comparatives

Comparative adjectives or adverbs are used to compare two places or things. For most adjectives or adverbs, add **-er** to form the comparative.

> Sam is a **tall** boy, but his brother is **taller**.

> I can run **fast**, but Lupita runs **faster**.

For other adjectives or adverbs, you may need to change the spelling to form the comparative.

> If a word ends in **-y**, change the **y** to **i** and then add **-er**: **pretty / prettier**.

> If a word ends in **-e**, just add **-r**: **late / later**.

> If a word ends in a single vowel and a single consonant, double the consonant and add **-er**: **big / bigger**.

Write the comparative form of the underlined adjective or adverb on the line to correctly complete the sentence. You may need to change the spelling.

1. Suzanne and Celia are <u>hard</u> workers, but Celia works _____.

2. This summer is <u>rainy</u>, but last summer was _____.

3. Tory likes <u>sweet</u> apples. Which one is _____—the green or the red?

4. My dog is <u>large</u>, but my friend's dog is even _____.

5. My sister can only swim in <u>shallow</u> water. Which end of the pool is _____?

6. I knew the movie would be <u>grim</u>, but it was _____ than I expected!

7. The people at school were <u>friendly</u>, but the people at this one are even _____.

   Grammar, Spelling & Vocabulary Activity Book • © Benchmark Education Company, LLC

Superlatives

Superlative adjectives or adverbs are used to compare three or more people, places, or things. For most adjectives or adverbs add **-est** to form the superlative. The spelling changes that apply to forming comparatives also apply to forming superlatives.

I want a **healthy** puppy. Which is the **healthiest** in the litter?

I also want a **big** puppy. That tan puppy looks like the **biggest**.

My dad is **wise**, but my grandfather is the **wisest** person I know.

Write the superlative form of the underlined word on the line to correctly complete the sentence. You may need to change the spelling.

1. I have been to many <u>noisy</u> concerts, but this is the _____.

2. Dad needs a <u>sharp</u> knife. He asked me to get the _____ we have.

3. I like <u>hot</u> sauce! Which of these is the _____?

4. That building is <u>tall</u>. It is the _____ building I have ever seen.

5. You were so <u>brave</u>! That was the _____ thing you have done.

6. Of all the <u>sad</u> books I have read, this one is the _____.

7. The kittens are so <u>little</u>. I want the _____ one!

Comparatives and Superlatives

Some comparative and superlative adjectives and adverbs are irregular. For example:

	Comparative	**Superlative**
good	better	best
bad	worse	worst

Use **more** and **most** to form the comparative and superlative of many longer words:

	Comparative	**Superlative**
carefully	more carefully	most carefully
generous	more generous	most generous

Circle the comparative or superlative that correctly completes each sentence. Write the word(s) on the line.

1. Yesterday, I saw the _____ movie I have ever seen!
most bad   worst

2. Which are the _____—the peaches, the grapes, or the plums?   most delicious   more delicious

3. The president is the _____ official in government.
more important   most important

4. I am much _____ at singing than dancing.
better   best

5. My red and blue shirt is _____ than my white one.
most colorful   more colorful

6. This bike is _____ than the other.
most expensive   more expensive

Possessives

Possessive nouns show that something belongs to one or more people, places, or things.

Use **'s** to show possession for one person, place, or thing—**Ann's** coat.

Use **s'** to show possession for more than one person, place, or thing—the **farmers'** crops.

Use **'s** to show possession for nouns with irregular plural forms—the **men's** team.

Replace the underlined words in each sentence with a possessive phrase. Write the possessive phrase on the line.

1. The <u>seats in the theater</u> are very uncomfortable.

_____

2. Long ago, <u>the hats that belonged to women</u> were fancy.

_____

3. The <u>uniforms of the teams</u> are different.

_____

4. The <u>legs of the tables</u> are wobbly.

_____

5. I found <u>a sweater belonging to Sally</u>.

_____

6. This is <u>the car belonging to my parents</u>.

_____

Pronoun-Antecedent Agreement

The noun that a pronoun replaces is called an antecedent. A pronoun and its antecedent must match in number (one or more than one) and gender (male or female).

Repetitious: Maria lost **Maria's** scarf, but **Maria** found it at the end of the day.

Better: Maria lost **her** scarf, but **she** found it at the end of the day.

In the example, **Maria**, **her**, and **she** match because they all refer to one girl.

Circle the pronoun that correctly matches its antecedent. Underline the antecedent. Write the pronoun on the line.

1. Louis went to see _____ grandmother after school.

    her   his   their

2. The girls will play _____ first game on Saturday.

    its   his   their

3. Will you please wash the dishes and put _____ away?

    our   them   her

4. I will do my homework now and hand _____ in tomorrow.

    it   he   them

5. Pedro is leaving soon. I will really miss _____.

    him   her   them

6. Ana, please put _____ books away so I don't trip on them!

    me   you   your

Grammar, Spelling & Vocabulary Activity Book • © Benchmark Education Company, LLC   G3 U5 W1 BLM1

Punctuate Dialogue

In dialogue, quotation marks set off a speaker's exact words. If the speaker is identified before the dialogue, place a comma before the first quotation mark after the speaker's tag. Place periods inside quotation marks. If the speaker is identified after the dialogue, place a comma inside the final quotation mark. If the dialogue itself ends in a question mark or exclamation point, place it inside the final quotation mark and drop the comma.

Coach Miller said, "You are late."

"Why are you late again?" asked Coach Miller.

"I'm really sorry," apologized Antoine. "I missed the bus."

Rewrite each sentence with correct punctuation.

1. Can you help me make dinner? Samir asked.

_____

2. Sorry, I can't help you David answered. I have to study.

_____

3. I want to see the new animated movie. Do you? asked Shieda.

_____

4. I do replied Justine. It looks really exciting!

_____

5. It looks as if it might rain said Mrs. Smith.

_____

6. I hope not replied Mr. Smith. I left my umbrella at home.

_____

Name _____ Date _____

Irregular Verbs

A regular verb ends in **-ed** or **-d** in the past tense. Irregular verbs, however, do not follow this rule. The spelling of irregular verbs can change in many different ways between the present and past tense forms.

Present Tense	Past Tense
grow	grew
make	made
find	found
get	got
buy	bought
is	are

grow	make	grew	made	found
find	get	buy	got	bought

Choose the correct present or past tense verb from the box to complete each sentence. Write the verb on the line.

1. Nina _____ three inches in the last year.

2. James and Janis _____ dinner for their parents.

3. I _____ my sister a gift with the money I saved.

4. I misplaced your book and have not _____ it yet.

5. I _____ sick after I went out without a coat.

6. Who _____ these wonderful tomatoes?

7. I need to _____ my notebook.

Name _____ Date _____

Irregular Verbs

Some verbs are irregular and do not follow any spelling rules for forming the plural or past tense of the verb. The verbs **to be** and **have** are examples of irregular verbs.

	to be			have	
Subject	**Present**	**Past**	**Subject**	**Present**	**Past**
Singular			**Singular**		
I	am	was	I	have	had
you	are	were	you	have	had
he/she/it	is	was	he/she/it	has	had
Plural			**Plural**		
we	are	were	we	have	had
they	are	were	they	have	had

Circle the correct form of the verb in ( ). Write the complete sentence on the line.

1. Dana (is   are) coming over today.

_____

2. I (am   was) getting some snacks ready now.

_____

3. John and Jill (was   were) here earlier.

_____

4. Do you (have   had) a piece of paper?

_____

5. I (is   am) not feeling well at all.

_____

Irregular Verbs

Some verbs are irregular. They do not follow the normal rules for forming plurals or tenses.

Circle the verb in ( ) that completes the sentence correctly.

1. My parents (buyed   bought) me a new bike for my birthday.

2. They (found   finded) the exact bike I wanted.

3. The bike (is   are) not new, but I love it.

4. I (growed   grew) out of my old bike last summer.

5. Who (got   getted) your bike for you?

6. We (is   are) both so lucky to have bikes!

7. Our parents (made   maked) us so happy.

8. I (have   had) fun riding my bike yesterday.

9. Jenna (rided   rode) her bike, too.

10. We (went   go) to the park before lunch.

11. We (sit   sat) on a bench and (drink drank) smoothies.

12. Jenna decided to (leave   left) early.

Irregular Verbs

Some verbs are irregular. They do not follow the normal rules for forming plurals or tenses.

Choose the correct verb from the box to complete each sentence. Write the verb on the line.

am	was	were	make
made	grew	found	had

1. We _____ a softball game last Saturday.

2. I _____ my own uniform.

3. Roberta _____ the pitcher last year.

4. This year, I _____ pitching.

5. The ball got lost, but then the outfielder _____ it.

6. Saturday, we _____ not able to bat very well.

Rewrite the sentence using the past tense of the underlined verb.

7. My sister <u>grows</u> many kinds of flowers.

_____

8. The bakery <u>makes</u> two kinds of pie.

_____

Punctuate Dialogue

When writing dialogue, use quotation marks and a comma to separate the speaker's words from the rest of the sentence. The first word in the quotation marks should begin with a capital letter. However, if the speaker's words are interrupted, do not capitalize the first word in the continuation of the dialogue. If a quotation is a question, the question mark is placed inside the final quotation mark and the comma is dropped.

"How many children are in your family?" asked Ms. Santiago. Will explained, "I am the youngest of three brothers."

"I have two sisters," Marta said, "and one brother."

Rewrite each sentence using correct punctuation and capitalization.

1. Andre complained There are too many leaves to rake.

   _____

2. Would you like some help? asked Beto.

   _____

3. Marta groaned I feel really sick.

   _____

4. Why did you like that book? Peter asked.

   _____

5. I was born in India Sanjay explained. Where are you from?

   _____

Possessives

Possessives show that something belongs to one or more persons, places, or things.

Use **'s** to show that something belongs to one person, place, or thing.

    Billy's shoes got wet.

    Our **class's teacher** is kind.

Use **s'** to show that something belongs to more than one person, place, or thing.

    All the **cars' lights** are on.

Rewrite each sentence, replacing the underlined words with a possessive phrase.

1. The <u>seats on the bus</u> are really uncomfortable.

_____

2. You can borrow <u>the bike that belongs to my sister</u>.

_____

3. I mow <u>the lawns of my neighbors</u>.

_____

4. This is the <u>table for the children</u>.

_____

5. <u>The rules of my boss</u> are tough but fair.

_____

Comparatives and Superlatives

Comparative adjectives or adverbs compare two places or things. Superlative adjectives or adverbs compare three or more places or things. Most comparatives end in **-er**, while most superlatives end in **-est**. For longer adjectives or adverbs, use the word **more** to form the comparative and the word **most** to form the superlative. Some comparatives and superlatives, however, are irregular and do not follow any of these patterns. For example:

	Comparative	Superlative
good	better	best
bad	worse	worst

Write the comparative form of the underlined word on the line to correctly complete the sentence.

1. The brown puppy is <u>adorable</u>, but the white one is

   _____.

2. This blanket is <u>cozy</u>, but that blanket is even _____!

3. I enjoy a <u>good</u> book. Which of these two is _____?

Write the superlative form of the underlined word on the line to correctly complete the sentence.

4. Some ski trails are <u>dangerous</u>. Which one is _____?

5. I am so <u>happy</u>! This is the _____ I've ever been!

6. This table is <u>large</u>, but that table is the _____!

Grammar, Spelling & Vocabulary Activity Book • © Benchmark Education Company, LLC   G3 U6 W2 BLM1

Pronoun-Antecedent Agreement

Writers use pronouns to replace the repetition of a noun. The noun that a pronoun replaces is called an antecedent. A pronoun and its antecedent must match in number (one or more than one) and gender (male or female).

Repetitive: Sergio went to **Sergio's** class, and **Sergio** sat in **Sergio's** seat.

Better: Sergio went to **his** class, and **he** sat in **his** seat.

Read each sentence. On the line, write a pronoun from the box that matches the antecedent of the sentence.

you	your	he	him	she
her	they	their	we	our

1. Aaron, will _____ please stop bothering me?

2. Dmitri and Sasha are going to help _____ dad paint.

3. I will take care of my sister when _____ wakes up.

4. Katie and I are best friends, so _____ do everything together.

5. I tried to call Luis, but I can't reach _____ .

6. Michelle, is this _____ backpack?

Name _____ Date _____

Concrete and Abstract Nouns

Concrete nouns are things you can see, hear, smell, touch, or taste, such as **classroom**, **teacher**, **pizza**, **music**, and **sidewalk**.

Abstract nouns are things that you cannot perceive with one of your five senses, such as **courage**, **fear**, **curiosity**, **hope**, and **kindness**.

Determine whether each noun in the box is concrete or abstract. Write the noun in the correct column of the chart below.

generosity	laughter	talent	aroma	shadow
loyalty	friendship	headache	artist	patience

Concrete Nouns	Abstract Nouns

Grammar, Spelling & Vocabulary Activity Book • © Benchmark Education Company, LLC   G3 U6 W3 BLM1

Name _____ Date _____

Irregular Verbs

Most regular past tense verbs ends in **-ed**. Irregular past tense verbs, however, do not follow any special spelling patterns. Some examples of verbs and their irregular past tense forms include **keep/kept**, **find/found**, **buy/bought**, **make/made**, and **to be/was**.

Write the past tense form of the verb in ( ) to complete each sentence.

1. I _____ three inches in the last year.   (grow)

2. I _____ that most of my clothes were too small. (find)

3. My mom _____ me some new things at the mall. (buy)

4. That _____ me very happy!   (make)

5. I _____ my new sweater yesterday.   (wear)

6. It _____ so cold outside.   (to be)

7. My sweater _____ me warm.   (keep)

Reciprocal Pronouns

Reciprocal pronouns help eliminate repetitive sentences or repetition within a sentence. Use the reciprocal pronoun **each other** to show that two people or things are performing the same action toward each other. Use the reciprocal pronoun **one another** to refer to three or more people or things.

They smiled at **each other**.

The teachers and students respect **one another**.

Rewrite the sentence or sentences using *each other* or *one another*.

1. Matt will meet Lin at the movies. Lin will meet Matt at the movies.

_____

2. My dog loves my cat, and my cat loves my dog.

_____

3. All the tourists stared at the monkeys, and all the monkeys stared at the tourists.

_____

4. Ken passed the ball to Juan. Juan passed the ball to Ken.

_____

5. The members of the band thanked the fans, and the fans thanked the members of the band.

_____

Reciprocal Pronouns

Use the reciprocal pronoun **each other** to refer to two people or things performing the same action toward each other. Use the reciprocal pronoun **one another** to refer to three or more people or things.

Luiz and Jon were happy to see **each other**.

We and all the visitors greeted **one another**.

Write the reciprocal pronoun that correctly completes the sentence: *each other* **or** *one another*.

1. My sister and my mom look just like _____.

2. All the boats in the harbor were bumping against _____ in the storm.

3. When you meet a new classmate, you should tell _____ your names.

4. Can we all agree to get along with _____?

5. The team members shook hands with _____ after the game.

6. I cannot believe it has been one whole year since we have seen _____.

Standard English

In writing, we use the conventions of standard English, which include complete sentences and proper vocabulary, and correct grammar, and punctuation. When we speak to one another or write dialogue in a story, we often bend the rules by using sentence fragments, slang, idioms, contractions, and everyday vocabulary.

Standard: Rosa was very excited to visit her grandmother.
Not Standard: Rosa was gonna see her grandmother.

Rewrite each sentence replacing any underlined word or phrase with the correct standard English word or phrase from the box.

going on	Are you	hurry up	any
going to	have to	I will see you later	

1. "If you don't <u>move it</u>, we're <u>gonna</u> be late!"

_____

2. "I can't eat <u>no</u> more!" groaned Mia.

_____

3. "What's <u>up</u> with Albert?"

_____

4. "<u>You</u> kidding me?"

_____

5. "I <u>gotta</u> go. <u>Catch you later</u>!"

_____

Simple, Complex, and Compound Sentences

A simple sentence has one subject and one verb. A compound sentence consists of two simple sentences joined by a comma and a coordinating conjunction, such as **and, or, but,** or **so**. A complex sentence joins a simple sentence and a fragment that cannot stand alone with a subordinating conjunction such as **although, because, since,** or **when.**

Simple: Mina excels at science.

Compound: Mina excels at science, **so** she may become a doctor.

Complex: Mina may become a doctor **because** she excels at science.

Underline whether each sentence is simple, compound, or complex. Circle the conjunction in the compound and complex sentences.

1. My mother is an immigrant from Haiti, but my father was born in California.
   simple   compound   complex

2. My classmates come from many countries.
   simple   compound   complex

3. I understand Creole, although we speak English at home.
   simple   compound   complex

4. My family is diverse, so we have Haitian and American traditions.
   simple   compound   complex

5. I am happy because we celebrate many different holidays, too!
   simple   compound   complex

Parts of Speech

The part of speech of a word reveals how the word is meant to be used in a sentence.		
Part of Speech	**Purpose**	**Examples**
Noun	name of a person, place, thing, or idea	Lisa likes **geography**.
Pronoun	takes the place of a noun	I will see **you** later.
Verb	links the subject of a sentence to more information about the subject; tells what the subject is doing	Peter is a great swimmer. We **are** proud of him.

He **swims** every day. |
| **Adjective** | describes nouns and pronouns | Today is **very** cold. |
| **Adverb** | describes verbs or adjectives | We have to walk **quickly**. |

Read each sentence. Write the part of speech for the underlined word.

1. Sam woke up and <u>looked</u> at his clock. _____

2. <u>He</u> was late for practice! _____

3. He had already been late <u>many</u> times this month. _____

4. Sam's <u>mom</u> said, "Don't worry. You are only a little late."

_____

5. Sam got dressed <u>quickly</u>. _____

6. He ran as fast as possible and <u>arrived</u> on time! _____

Name _____ Date _____

Linking Words to Create Compound and Complex Sentences

Conjunctions link the parts of a compound or a complex sentence. Use a comma and a coordinating conjunction such as **and, or, but,** or **so** to create a compound sentence. Use a subordinating conjunction such as **although, because, since,** or **unless** to create a complex sentence.

Compound: Ben loves to act**, and** he will be in our play.

Complex: Ben will be in our play **because** he loves to act.

Rewrite each pair of simple sentences to form a compound sentence using the conjunction in ( ) and a comma.

1. My sister is good at math. I am good at science.   (and)

_____

2. It's a very long walk to school. I take the bus.   (so)

_____

3. Maria plays soccer. She would rather play basketball.   (but)

_____

Rewrite each pair of simple sentences to form a complex sentence using the conjunction in ( ).

4. Our soccer game ended. Then it started to rain.   (before)

_____

5. We will also play tomorrow. We won't if the field is wet. (unless)

_____

Reciprocal Pronouns

Use the reciprocal pronouns **each other** or **one another** when two or more people or things are performing the same action and are both affected by the action in the same way. **Each other** refers to two people or things. **One another** refers to three or more people or things.

Bella and Drew smiled at **each other.**

After the game, the players on both teams high-fived **one another.**

Rewrite each sentence using *each other* or *one another*.

1. Kitta admired Manuel, and Manuel admired Kitta.

_____

2. Each artist complimented all the other artists.

_____

3. My mom usually agrees with my dad, and my dad usually agrees with my mom.

_____

4. My dog gets along with my two cats. My two cats get along with my dog.

_____

5. Ana took turns writing to Sumiko. Sumiko took turns writing to Ana.

_____

Parts of Speech

The part of speech of a word tells how a word is meant to be used in speaking or writing, as a noun, pronoun, verb, adjective, or adverb.

Part of Speech	Example
Nouns:	**Alexa** loves **burgers.**
Pronouns:	Will **you** text **me** later?
Verbs:	Dan **is** an avid reader.
	His parents **are** proud of him.
	He **reads** two books a week.
Adjectives:	It has been so **hot** and **dry**.
Adverbs:	I **really** wish it would rain.

Read each sentence. Circle the part of speech for the underlined word. Then circle another word in the sentence that is that same part of speech.

1. Nina is a great hitter, but <u>she</u> needs to work on her catching.

   noun   pronoun

2. Ruth can throw and <u>catch</u> the ball very well.

   verb   adjective

3. Maybe <u>Ruth</u> and Nina can practice together.

   adverb   noun

4. Do you like our new <u>yellow</u> shirts?

   adverb   adjective

5. My shirt fits <u>poorly</u> and stains easily.

   adverb   noun

6. I hope it's less dirty after I <u>wash</u> it.

   adjective   verb

Name _____ Date _____

Simple, Compound, and Complex Sentences

A simple sentence has one subject and one verb. A compound sentence consists of two simple sentences joined by a comma and a linking word, such as **and**, **or**, **but**, or **so**. A complex sentence consists of a simple sentence and a fragment, joined together using a linking word such as **although**, **because**, **since**, **unless**, **before**, or **when**.

  Simple: Sam waited for the bus.
  Compound: Sam waited for the bus, **but** it was late.
  Complex: Sam waited for the bus **although** it was late.

Underline whether each sentence is simple, compound, or complex. Then circle the linking word in each compound and complex sentence.

1. I love banana bread, so my aunt often makes it for me.
simple   compound   complex

2. Several of my neighbors have pets.
simple   compound   complex

3. I enjoy walking my next-door neighbor's dog unless it
is raining.
simple   compound   complex

4. My neighbor across the street also has a dog, and I walk
that one, too.
simple   compound   complex

5. I usually walk the dogs in the afternoon before I start my
homework.
simple   compound   complex

   Grammar, Spelling & Vocabulary Activity Book • © Benchmark Education Company, LLC   G3 U8 W2 BLM1

Linking Words to Create Compound and Complex Sentences

Conjunctions link the simple sentences or clauses that make up the parts of a compound or a complex sentence. Use a comma and a coordinating conjunction such as **and**, **or**, **but**, or **so** to create a compound sentence. Use a subordinating conjunction such as **although**, **because**, **since**, or **unless** to create a complex sentence.

Compound sentence: Kim likes to play basketball, **but** she likes baseball more.

Complex sentence: Let's meet at the pool **unless** it rains.

Choose a coordinating conjunction from the box to complete each compound sentence.

and	but	or	so

1. Ramona ate lunch late, _____ she wasn't hungry for dinner.

2. Fred is an excellent dancer, _____ he is a good singer, too.

Choose a subordinating conjunction from the box to complete each complex sentence.

although	because	until	since	unless

3. I will be in the race _____ I'm not a very fast runner.

4. I kept eating grapes _____ there were none left.

5. Carlos will join the team _____ practice conflicts with his piano lessons.

6. I asked Mom to pick up some snacks _____ we were so hungry!

Past Tense Verbs

To form the past tense of regular verbs, follow the rules in the chart below.

For most regular verbs, add **-ed** to the end of the verb.	paint + **ed**	painted
If a verb ends in **-e**, just add **-d**.	introduce + **d**	introduced
If a verb ends in a vowel and a single consonant, double the consonant and add **-ed**.	refer + **r** + **ed**	referred
If a verb ends in a consonant and **-y**, change the **-y** to **-i** and add **-ed**.	study studi + **ed**	studied

Fill in the blank in each sentence with the past tense form of the verb in ( ). Then write the complete sentence on the line.

1. My sister _____ to five colleges. (apply)

_____

2. Our dad _____ her with her applications. (help)

_____

3. She _____ with joy when she was accepted! (cry)

_____

4. She _____ that she wouldn't get in. (worry)

_____

5. I _____ her because I was so happy! (hug)

_____

Past Tense Verbs

Most past tense verbs end with **-ed**. Some verbs, however, are irregular and do not follow this pattern. Some examples of irregular verbs include **to be/was**, **have/had**, **find/found**, **grow/grew**, **buy/bought**, **get/got**, and **make/made**.

Circle the verb in ( ) that correctly completes the sentence. Then write the verb on the line.

1. My friends and I _____ cookies yesterday. (maked made)

2. They _____ really delicious. (were is)

3. Lila's mom _____ the ingredients for us. (get got)

4. She _____ almost everything at the market down the street. (bought buyed)

5. She _____ to go to another store for the flour. (had haved)

6. Luckily, she _____ it! (finded found)

7. We _____ a lot of vegetables. (grew growed)

8. My brother _____ really glad when I gave him one! (was be)

Abstract Nouns

Concrete nouns are things that you can see, hear, smell, taste, or touch, such as **pizza**, **cloud**, and **friend**.
Abstract nouns are things or ideas that cannot be perceived with one of your five senses. **Hunger**, **loyalty**, and **democracy** are examples of abstract nouns.

Complete each sentence with an abstract noun from the box.

patriotism	weather	wisdom	generosity
independence	vacation	pleasure	disagreements

1. Mr. Chen paid me more than he needed to. His _____ is overwhelming!

2. My family is going to the beach for _____ —I can't wait!

3. I hope that the _____ on Tuesday will be warm and sunny.

4. We fly a flag on the fourth of July to show our _____.

5. On the 4th, Americans celebrate the country's _____.

6. My brother and I have our _____ but we still love each other.

7. I like cooking and get _____ from doing it.

8. My sister often gives me advice, she has a deep _____ about things.

Name _____ Date _____

Abstract Nouns

Abstract nouns are things or ideas that cannot be perceived with one of our five senses or something you cannot see, hear, smell, taste, or touch. **Kindness**, **honesty**, and **despair** are examples of abstract nouns.

Underneath each sentence is a concrete noun and an abstract noun. Circle the abstract noun and then write it on the line to complete the sentence.

1. I often think fondly about my _____.

    grandmother   childhood

2. My parents think that it's important to have _____.

    compassion   possessions

3. I think it's important to have my parents' _____.

    trust   computer

4. I am in awe of my teacher's _____.

    car   brilliance

5. I study dinosaurs to expand my _____ of them.

    knowledge   collection

6. I give half of my allowance to my favorite _____.

    cousin   charity

7. My grandfather says that I bring him great _____.

    cookies   joy

Simple, Complex, and Compound Sentences

A simple sentence has one subject and one verb. A complex sentence has two subjects and two verbs, plus a linking word such as **because**, **unless**, **after**, **until**, or **although**.

A compound sentence has two subjects and two verbs, a comma, and a linking word such as **and**, **or**, **but**, or **so**.

Simple Sentences: Ben likes most kinds of pizza. He doesn't care for olives.

Compound Sentence: Ben loves most kinds of pizza, **but** he doesn't care for olives.

Complex Sentence: Ben likes most kinds of pizza **although** he doesn't care for olives.

Underline whether each sentence is simple, complex, or compound. Then circle the linking word in each complex and compound sentence.

1. I might be an engineer someday, or I might be an architect.

simple   complex   compound

2. Mira will stay in the library until her mother picks her up.

simple   complex   compound

3. Eduardo will dry the dishes after his sister washes them.

simple   complex   compound

4. Maryann will shop for a new coat on Saturday.

simple   complex   compound

5. I will help Amar with math, so he will do well on his test.

simple   complex   compound

Name _____ Date _____

Comparatives and Superlatives

There are three ways to form comparatives and superlatives using adjectives and adverbs.

1. Add **-er** or **-est** to the end of the adjective or adverb.

	Comparative	Superlative
small	smaller	smallest

2. For longer adjectives or adverbs, add **more** or **most** in front of the word.

	Comparative	Superlative
artistic	more artistic	most artistic

3. Some comparatives and superlatives are irregular and do not follow a pattern. For example:

	Comparative	Superlative
good	better	best

Write the comparative or superlative of the word in ( ) to complete each sentence. You may need to change the spelling of the word.

1. Which of these two books did you like _____? (good)

2. That is the _____ dog I have ever seen! (tiny)

3. The brown chair is much _____ than the red one. (comfortable)

4. That's the _____ I've ever done on a test! (bad)

5. My uncle Pedro is the _____ person I know. (wise)

6. I'm _____ in age to my older brother than my younger one. (close)

7. Cabbage is the _____ food I've ever tasted! (disgusting)

Comparatives and Superlatives

There are three ways to form comparatives or superlatives from adjectives or adverbs.

1. Add **-er** or **-est** to the end of the adjective or adverb.
2. For longer adjectives or adverbs, add **more** or **most** in front of the word.
3. Some are irregular and do not follow a pattern. For example: good, better, best.

Circle the incorrect word in each sentence. Write the correct comparative or superlative on the line.

1. I think your explanation is confusinger than mine.

_____

2. These are the beautifulest flowers in the shop.

_____

3. Which yogurt do you think is gooder—strawberry or vanilla?

_____

4. A storm on field day? This is the baddest day ever!

_____

5. Who is your goodest friend at school?

_____

6. I'm embarrasseder now than I was before.

_____

7. These jeans are the comfortablest pair I have.

_____

Verb Tenses

To form the past tense of most verbs add **-ed** or **-d** to the end of the verb. Some verbs, however, are irregular and do not follow this spelling pattern. An irregular verb has a special spelling in the past tense. Some irregular verbs include **have/had**, **grow/grew**, **find/found**, and **make/made**.

Rewrite each sentence, replacing the underlined verb with the past tense form. There is a mix of regular and irregular verbs.

1. We <u>will have</u> our first basketball game on Friday.

_____

2. We <u>are</u> the number one team in the league.

_____

3. I <u>am</u> the center and team captain.

_____

4. Julia <u>makes</u> all her foul shots.

_____

5. Julia <u>hopes</u> to be the team captain.

_____

6. She <u>will grow</u> four inches taller in a year!

_____

7. Julia and I <u>find</u> that it helps to be tall.

_____

Name _____ Date _____

Irregular Comparatives and Superlatives

Comparative adjectives or adverbs compare two places or things. Superlative adjectives or adverbs compare three or more places or things. Most comparatives end in **-er**, while most superlatives end in **-est**. For longer adjectives or adverbs, use the word **more** to form the comparative and the word **most** to form the superlative. Some comparatives and superlatives, however, are irregular and do not follow any of these patterns. For example: **good**, **better**, **best** or **bad**, **worse**, **worst**.

Complete each sentence by writing the correct comparative or superlative form of the word in ( ) on the line.

1. There are so many choices! Which kind of pizza do you like

_____? (good)

2. I like both pepperoni and veggie pizza, but I like veggie

_____. (good)

3. I think this striped scarf is _____ than the

plaid one. (attractive)

4. That's the _____ scarf in the store! (ugly)

5. Ms. Ramirez is the _____ teacher in my

school. (popular)

6. That was not a good game, but last week's game was

_____. (bad)

Grammar, Spelling & Vocabulary Activity Book • © Benchmark Education Company, LLC   G3 U10 W1 BLM1

Name _____ Date _____

Irregular Verb Tenses

A regular verb is one that uses **-ed** or **-d** to form the past tense. Some verbs are irregular, however, and do not follow the normal rules for forming tenses. The verbs **find, grow, buy, get,** and **make** have irregular past tenses. The verbs **have** and **to be** have irregular present and past tenses.

Write the correct form of the verb in ( ) to complete each sentence.

1. We _____ a foot of snow on the first day of spring last year. (get)

2. My mom woke me up late because I _____ no school. (have)

3. Shelley and I _____ a huge snowman in the park. (make)

4. We _____ two branches for the snowman's arms. (find)

5. The branches _____ already on the ground. (to be)

6. That spring, the crocuses _____ right through the snow! (grow)

7. It was lucky that my dad just _____ a new shovel. (buy)

8. Today is the first day of spring this year, and it _____ warm and sunny. (to be)

9. I _____ happy about that! (to be)

Standard English

When we write, we use the conventions of standard English, which include complete sentences and standardized vocabulary, grammar, and punctuation. When we speak or write informally to one another, or write dialogue in a story, we often bend the rules by using sentence fragments, slang, idioms, contractions, and everyday vocabulary.

Read the letter that Mike wrote to his friend Alison. Imagine that Mike was writing a formal letter instead. Using the same information, rewrite the letter to better represent the conventions of standard English.

Hey, Ali!!! Week 2 at camp is AWESOME!! All the kids are super cool, and I feel like we're already best friends. This week we got to go camping in the woods, I thought it would be scary but we all sang so many songs and ran around and it was the best. Next week we're gonna ride horses! I'll let you know how that goes, I bet it'll be awesome too. —Mike

_____
_____
_____
_____
_____
_____
_____
_____
_____

Punctuate Dialogue

In dialogue, quotation marks set off a speaker's exact words. If the speaker is identified before the dialogue, place a comma after the speaker's tag before the first quotation mark. Place periods inside quotation marks. If the speaker is identified after the dialogue, place a comma inside the quotation marks. If the dialogue itself includes a question mark or exclamation point, place it inside the quotation marks. Drop the comma.

   Liz yawned and said, "I'm too tired to read another page."
   "I'm going to bed, too," agreed Hannah. "What time is it?"

Read each sentence. Then rewrite it correctly on the line.

1. What time is the concert? Simone asked.

_____

2. It starts at 7 o'clock answered Violet. But let's get there early.

_____

3. Mom asked How many friends will be sleeping over?

_____

4. Only Miguel and Samuel said Amar. Is that okay?

_____

5. What time will you be home today? asked Dad.

_____

6. Tomas replied I should be home right after school.

_____

Parts of Speech

Part of Speech	Examples
Nouns:	**Aaron** is going to the **beach**.
Pronouns:	Can **I** go with **him**?
Verbs:	Petra **was** here last week.
	Her sisters **were** with her.
Adjectives:	The painting is **beautiful**.
Adverbs:	You must study it **carefully**.

Complete the story by writing a word that matches the part of speech in parentheses ( ) below each line.

Last summer, my _____ and _____ went to
            (noun)   (pronoun)

_____ for _____ days. We looked for the
  (noun)   (adjective)

_____ where we would stay. We _____
  (noun)   (verb)

_____ down a dark and _____ road.
  (adverb)   (adjective)

We finally _____ it in the middle of the _____
        (verb)   (adjective)

_____! When my _____ opened the door,
  (noun)   (noun)

_____ _____ very _____!
 (pronoun)   (verb)   (adverb)

"It's a _____!" _____ _____. It was so
    (noun)   (pronoun)   (verb)

_____! We _____ and _____! That was
 (adjective)   (verb)   (verb)

just the start of the _____ vacation ever!
          (comparative adjective)

Adjectives and Adverbs

Adjectives: Describe or tell more about nouns and pronouns. Some examples of adjectives include **three, pleasant, windy, harmful,** and **amazing**.

Adverbs: Describe or tell more about verbs, adjectives, and other adverbs. Some examples of adverbs include **cheerfully, carefully, often, soon,** and **very**.

Circle the adjective in each sentence. Underline the word it describes.

1. Sylvie's mother gave her a long list of things she needed.

2. Shopping was one of Sylvie's favorite activities.

3. She loved picking out the reddest berries.

4. She enjoyed choosing nutritious vegetables.

Circle the adverb in each sentence. Underline the word it describes.

5. Sylvie walked quickly through the store.

6. She wanted time to easily buy everything on the list!

7. Sylvie's mother trusts her completely to do the grocery shopping.

8. Sylvie is a very responsible girl!

Spelling & Vocabulary

Short Vowels

conflicts	examples	helpful	imagine
plans	printed	problems	upset

**Circle the spelling word that completes the sentence.
Write it on the line.**

1. You should talk to your friend if you are _____ with her.

printed   upset   helpful

2. _____ don't go away if you don't talk about them.

Problems   Examples   Plans

3. It's not always possible to avoid unpleasant _____.

examples   plans   conflicts

4. I like to _____ a world where everyone gets along.

helpful   imagine   upset

5. They _____ their names below their signatures.

printed   plans   conflicts

6. The architect presented his _____ for the new building.

upset   plans   imagine

7. The teacher provided the students with plenty of _____.

printed   examples   helpful

Name _____ Date _____

Short Vowels

conflicts	examples	helpful	imagine
plans	printed	problems	upset

Write the spelling words for the given number of syllables.

Spelling word with 1 syllable

1. _____

Spelling words with 2 syllables

2. _____   3. _____

4. _____   5. _____

6. _____

Spelling words with 3 syllables

7. _____   8. _____

Write the spelling word that is an antonym or a synonym of the bold word.

9. **pretend** synonym: _____

10. **clashes** synonym: _____

11. **happy** antonym: _____

12. **troubles** synonym: _____

Long a

became	explained	favored	plain
raised	separate	swayed	vain

Write the correct spelling word for each clue.

1. Someone who always looks in the mirror is this. _____

2. This is the opposite of **lowered**. _____

3. The candidate who won was this by more voters. _____

4. This is another word for **simple**. _____

5. You do this with clothes when you sort them for

washing. _____

6. Moved from side to side _____

7. It means "turned into." _____

8. Your teacher did this to help you understand something.

_____

Write the spelling word that completes each analogy.

9. Flavored is to **tasty** as **unflavored** is to _____.

10. Humble is to **modest** as **conceited** is to _____.

Long a

became	explained	favored	plain
raised	separate	swayed	vain

Write the spelling words for the given sound-spelling pattern.

Spelling words with long *a* spelled *a_e*

1. _____   2. _____

Spelling words with long *a* spelled *ai*

3. _____   4. _____

5. _____   6. _____

Spelling word with long *a* spelled *ay*

7. _____

Spelling word with long *a* spelled *a*

8. _____

Name _____ Date _____

Long o, Long u, and Long /oo/

arrows	broken	contribution	new
obeyed	told	united	used

Write the spelling word that goes with the other words.

1. hand-me-down, worn, _____

2. markers, pointers, _____

3. unused, fresh, _____

4. damaged, cracked, _____

5. said, spoke, _____

6. donation, gift, _____

7. together, in agreement, _____

8. complied, behaved, _____

Write a spelling word to complete each sentence.

9. If you follow the yellow _____, you will find

the office.

10. Our dog finally _____ when the trainer said, "Stay."

11. Did you bring your _____ to the food drive?

12. Our country is made up of fifty _____ states.

Long o, Long u, and Long /oo/

arrows	broken	contribution	new
obeyed	told	united	used

Write the spelling word for the given sound-spelling pattern.

Spelling words with long *o* spelled *o*

1. _____   2. _____

3. _____

Spelling word with long *o* spelled *ow*

4. _____

Spelling words with long *u* spelled *u*

5. _____   6. _____

7. _____

Spelling word with long *u* spelled *ew*

8. _____

Write the spelling word that is an antonym or a synonym of the bold word.

9. **divided** antonym: _____

10. **donation** synonym: _____

Name _____ Date _____

Long e

| even | freedom | honey | hungry |
| leave | pieces | queens | screamed |

Write the spelling word that completes each analogy.

1. **Dark** is to **light** as **arrive** is to _____.

2. **Parts** are to _____ as **basements** are to **cellars**.

3. **Starving** is to _____ as **boiling** is to **hot**.

4. **Men** are to **women** as **kings** are to _____.

5. **Bees** are to _____ as **cows** are to **milk**.

Write a spelling word to complete each sentence.

6. My dog loves his _____ when we let him run in the yard.

7. I don't like chocolate _____ though I have tried it many times.

8. Juliana _____ with fright during the scary movie.

Long e

| even | freedom | honey | hungry |
| leave | pieces | queens | screamed |

Write the spelling words for the given spelling pattern.

Spelling words with *ea*

1. _____ **2.** _____

Spelling words with *ee*

3. _____ **4.** _____

Spelling words with *y* or *ey*

5. _____ **6.** _____

Spelling word that has the *ie*

7. _____

Spelling word that has the *e*

8. _____

Write the spelling word that matches each definition.

9. depart _____ **10.** needing food _____

Long i

| cried | fighting | island | might |
| myself | provided | sacrifice | unwind |

Write a spelling word that goes with the other two words.

1. I, me, _____

2. can, could, _____

3. donated, gave, _____

4. unroll, untwist, _____

5. shouted, yelled, _____

6. peninsula, reef, _____

7. arguing, battling, _____

8. give up, lose, _____

Each sentence has an incorrect word. Circle the word. Then write the spelling word that makes the sentence correct.

9. Please stop frightening and make up. _____

10. An inland is surrounded by water. _____

11. I mite call you later. _____

12. She cured when I gave her the news. _____

13. The bakery proved muffins for our bake sale. _____

Long i

cried	fighting	island	might
myself	provided	sacrifice	unwind

Write the spelling words for the given number of letters.

Spelling words with 5 letters

1. _____ 2. _____

Spelling words with 6 letters

3. _____ 4. _____

5. _____

Spelling words with 8 letters

6. _____ 7. _____

Spelling words with 9 letters

8. _____

Write the spelling word that matches each definition.

9. in a battle _____ 10. donated _____

Compound Words

firelight	heartbeat	hillside	mountaintop
thunderclap	treetops	underwater	woodstove

Write a spelling word that goes with the other two words.

1. pulse, doctor, _____

2. warmth, winter, _____

3. lightning, rain, _____

4. leaves, nests, _____

5. camping, tents, _____

6. peak, summit, _____

7. wet, murky, _____

8. slope, rounded, _____

Fill in the boxes for the spelling word *firelight*.

meaning	sentence
compound words with *fire*	**compound words with *light***

firelight

Compound Words

firelight	heartbeat	hillside	mountaintop
thunderclap	treetops	underwater	woodstove

Write the spelling words for the given number of syllables.

Spelling words with 2 syllables

1. _____   2. _____

3. _____   4. _____

5. _____

Spelling words with 3 syllables

6. _____   7. _____

Spelling words with 4 syllables

8. _____

Write the spelling word that is an antonym or a synonym of the bold word.

9. **canyon** antonym: _____

10. **boom** synonym: _____

11. **immersed** synonym: _____

12. **pulse** synonym: _____

Name _____ Date _____

r-Controlled Vowels ar, or

Arctic	born	carnivores	forest
form	forward	shark	sharp

Write the spelling word that matches each definition.

1. large ocean fish that has many rows of teeth _____

2. a place where many trees grow _____

3. the area of land around the North Pole _____

4. straight ahead _____

5. animals that eat other animals _____

Circle the incorrect word in each sentence. Then write the spelling word that makes the sentence correct.

6. I was bone in Anchorage, Alaska. _____

7. Be careful with that shape knife. _____

8. Polar bears live in the attic. _____

9. Tigers are cavities. _____

10. Four lines of the same length from a square. _____

 Grammar, Spelling & Vocabulary Activity Book • © Benchmark Education Company, LLC   G3 U3 W1 BLM1

Name _____ Date _____

r-Controlled Vowels ar, or

Arctic	born	carnivores	forest
form	forward	shark	sharp

Write the spelling words for the given number of syllables.

Spelling words with 1 syllable

1. _____   2. _____

3. _____   4. _____

Spelling words with 2 syllables

5. _____   6. _____

7. _____

Spelling word with 3 syllables

8. _____

Write a spelling word to complete each sentence.

9. Some animals are herbivores, and some are _____.

10. Predators have strong jaws and _____teeth.

11. My mom always says, "I will never forget the day you were

    _____."

12. Please _____ two lines outside the auditorium.

r-Controlled Vowels er, ir, ur

birds	butterfly	caterpillar	curl
dangerous	deter	furry	survive

Write the spelling word that matches each definition.

1. Animals who live through the winter do this. _____

2. These animals lay eggs and have feathers. _____

3. This insect collects nectar from flowers. _____

4. This insect can transform into a butterfly. _____

5. To keep someone from doing something. _____

6. This describes kittens and bunnies. _____

Fill in the boxes for the spelling word _dangerous_.

meaning	sentence
example	**related words**
	noun: adverb: antonym:

dangerous

r-Controlled Vowels er, ir, ur

birds	butterfly	caterpillar	curl
dangerous	deter	furry	survive

Write the spelling words for the given number of syllables.

Spelling words with 1 syllable

1. _____ 2. _____

Spelling words with 2 syllables

3. _____ 4. _____

5. _____

Spelling words with 3 syllables

6. _____ 7. _____

Spelling word with 4 syllables

8. _____

Write the spelling word that is an antonym or a synonym of the bold word.

9. **harmless**   antonym: _____

10. **discourage**   synonym: _____

11. **shaggy**   synonym: _____

12. **die**   antonym: _____

Closed Syllables

better	black	blended	munching
predators	quickly	sticky	suddenly

Write a spelling word to complete each analogy.

1. **Green** is to **grass** as _____ is to **coal**.

2. **Separate** is to _____ as **sharp** is to **dull**.

3. **Uphill** is to **downhill** as _____ is to **worse**.

4. **Honey** is to _____ as **butter** is to **greasy**.

5. **Slowly** is to _____ as **crawling** is to **sprinting**.

6. _____ are to **prey** as **detectives** are to **suspects**.

7. **Milk** is to **sipping** as **popcorn** is to _____.

8. _____ is to **instantly** as **tossed** is to **threw**.

Write the spelling words that end with the suffix -y or -ly.

9. _____   10. _____

11. _____

Grammar, Spelling & Vocabulary Activity Book • © Benchmark Education Company, LLC   G3 U3 W3 BLM1

Closed Syllables

better	black	blended	munching
predators	quickly	sticky	suddenly

Write the spelling words for the given number of syllables.

Spelling word with 1 syllable

1. _____

Spelling words with 2 syllables

2. _____   3. _____

4. _____   5. _____

6. _____

Spelling words with 3 syllables

7. _____   8. _____

Write the spelling word that matches each definition.

9. all at once _____

10. of higher quality _____

11. merged _____

12. gummy _____

Open Syllables

apron	began	briars	lady
music	potatoes	replied	vocabulary

Write a spelling word to complete each analogy.

1. Boy is to **gentleman** as **girl** is to _____.

2. Vegetables are to _____ as **fruits** are to **apples**.

3. Chef is to _____ as **baby** is to **bib**.

4. Asked is to **queried** as **answered** is to _____.

5. Thorny is to _____ as **feathery** is to **grass**.

Write a spelling word to complete each sentence.

6. Julio _____ piano lessons when he was five years old.

7. Learning _____ is very important to Julio's family.

8. Having a good _____ helps you communicate well with others.

Open Syllables

apron	began	briars	lady
music	potatoes	replied	vocabulary

Write the spelling words for the given number of syllables.

Spelling words with 2 syllables

1. _____

2. _____

3. _____

4. _____

5. _____

6. _____

Spelling word with 3 syllables

7. _____

Spelling word with 5 syllables

8. _____

Write the spelling word that matches each definition.

9. words used or known by a person _____

10. worn while cooking to protect the clothes underneath

_____

11. what an orchestra plays _____

12. starchy vegetables _____

Consonant-le Syllables

able	bicycle	fable	gentle
gobble	purple	single	terrible

Write a spelling word that goes with the other two words.

1. scooter, tricycle, _____

2. one, alone, _____

3. story, myth, _____

4. tender, kindly, _____

5. red, blue, _____

6. devour, gulp, _____

7. awful, horrible, _____

8. ready, competent, _____

Each sentence has an incorrect word. Circle the word. Then write the spelling word that makes the sentence correct.

9. That is a lovely pupil sweater. _____

10. They had a trouble time at the event. _____

11. It's hard to not garble down a delicious meal. _____

12. I can't remember a singer thing about her. _____

13. You must be very grateful with the kitten. _____

Consonant-le Syllables

able	bicycle	fable	gentle
gobble	purple	single	terrible

Write the spelling words for the given number of letters.

Spelling word with 4 letters

1. _____

Spelling word with 5 letters

2. _____

Spelling words with 6 letters

3. _____

Spelling word with 6 letters

4. _____

5. _____

6. _____

Spelling word with 7 letters

7. _____

Spelling word with 8 letters

8. _____

Write a spelling word to complete each sentence.

9. I am _____ to make my own lunch.

10. I ride my _____ to school everyday.

11. My favorite color is _____.

12. I took a _____ cup from the pile.

Vowel Teams

beans	boaster	feet	green
shook	sprouted	too	week

Write a spelling word that goes with the other two words.

1. day, month, _____

2. arms, legs, _____

3. yellow, blue, _____

4. rattled, jiggled, _____

5. planted, watered, _____

6. bragger, show-off, _____

7. also, additionally, _____

8. seeds, grains, _____

Fill in the boxes for the spelling word *sprouted*.

meaning	sentence
example *sprouted*	**related words** noun: present tense verb: synonym:

Vowel Teams

beans	boaster	feet	green
shook	sprouted	too	week

Write the spelling words for the given number of letters.
Spelling word with 3 letters

1. _____

Spelling words with 4 letters

2. _____   3. _____

Spelling words with 5 letters

4. _____   5. _____

6. _____

Spelling word with 7 letters   **Spelling word with 8 letters**

7. _____   8. _____

Complete each sentence with a spelling word or words.

9. The ground _____ during the earthquake.

10. Brad is a _____ when he talks about his

basketball skills.

11. I am going to write one _____.

12. The soft, _____ grass feels good under my

_____.

Vowel-Consonant-e Syllables

arrive	broke	celebrated	wire
huge	June	telephone	whole

Write the spelling word that matches each definition.

1. the sixth month of the year _____

2. unbroken _____

3. a thin thread of metal _____

4. extremely large _____

5. get to a place _____

6. device used to speak with others _____

7. smashed into pieces _____

Fill in the boxes for the spelling word *celebrated*.

meaning	sentence
examples	**related words**
	noun: present tense verb: antonym:

celebrated

Grammar, Spelling & Vocabulary Activity Book • © Benchmark Education Company, LLC

Vowel-Consonant-e Syllables

arrive	broke	celebrated	wire
huge	June	telephone	whole

Write the spelling words for the given number of syllables.

Spelling words with 1 syllable

1. _____   2. _____

3. _____   4. _____

5. _____

Spelling word with 2 syllables   **Spelling word with 3 syllables**

6. _____   7. _____

Spelling word with 4 syllables

8. _____

Complete each sentence with a spelling word.

9. Let me give you my _____ number.

10. The _____ extends from the pole to the house.

11. Her plane will _____ at midnight.

12. Will the _____ class go on the field trip?

Vowel-r Syllables

clerk	coworkers	mother	over
performed	simpler	smaller	various

Write the spelling word that matches each definition.

1. People who do a job together are these. _____

2. The actor did this on stage. _____

3. If a question is this, it's easier to answer. _____

4. This is a female parent. _____

5. It's the opposite of *larger*. _____

6. A person who works in a shop is called this. _____

7. This is a word for "many different kinds." _____

8. This is the opposite of *under*. _____

Complete each analogy with a spelling word.

9. **Uncle** is to **aunt** as **father** is to _____.

10. **Siblings** are to **family** as _____ are to **office**.

Vowel-r Syllables

clerk	coworkers	mother	over
performed	simpler	smaller	various

Write the spelling word for the given number of letters.

Spelling word with 4 letters   **Spelling word with 5 letters**

1. _____   2. _____

Spelling word with 6 letters

3. _____

Spelling words with 7 letters

4. _____   5. _____

6. _____

Spelling words with 9 letters

7. _____   8. _____

Write the spelling word that is an antonym or a synonym of the bold word.

9. **under**   antonym: _____

10. **acted**   synonym: _____

11. **easier**   synonym: _____

12. **one**   antonym: _____

Inflectional Endings -ed, -ing

carried	changed	creating	introduced
relied	sharing	taking	using

Write a spelling word that goes with the other two words.

1. dividing, splitting, _____

2. depended, needed, _____

3. making, inventing, _____

4. hauled, lifted, _____

5. began, started, _____

6. transformed, altered, _____

7. operating, handling, _____

8. going, bringing, _____

Fill in the boxes for the spelling word *sharing*.

meaning	sentence
example	related words
	base word: past tense verb: future tense verb: antonym:

sharing

Inflectional Endings -ed, -ing

| carried | changed | creating | introduced |
| relied | sharing | taking | using |

Write the spelling word for the given inflectional ending.

Spelling words with *-ed*

1. _____
2. _____
3. _____
4. _____

Spelling words with *-ing*

5. _____
6. _____
7. _____
8. _____

Write a spelling word to complete each sentence.

9. My sister and I enjoy _____ our clothes with each other.

10. When I was first _____ to Adam, I did not know he was in my grade.

11. I _____ the groceries all the way home.

12. This hotel has _____ so much since I last stayed here.

Name _____ Date _____

Irregular Plurals

geese	grass	lives	people
sheep	teeth	themselves	wolves

Write the spelling word that matches each clue.

1. These animals live in packs. _____

2. Some animals graze on this. _____

3. We use these to chew our food. _____

4. People make wool out of the fur of these animals. _____

5. Cats are said to have nine of these. _____

Circle the incorrect word in each sentence. Then write the spelling word that makes the sentence correct.

6. There are so many purple at the meeting. _____

7. The honking of the guests is so loud. _____

8. Vain people think highly of thresholds. _____

9. The gross is still wet from the rain. _____

10. A herd of shapes is in the pasture. _____

 Grammar, Spelling & Vocabulary Activity Book • © Benchmark Education Company, LLC

Name _____ Date _____

Irregular Plurals

geese	grass	lives	people
sheep	teeth	themselves	wolves

Write the correct spelling words for the given number of letters.

Spelling words with 5 letters

1. _____   2. _____

3. _____   4. _____

5. _____

Spelling words with 6 letters

6. _____   7. _____

Spelling word with 10 letters

8. _____

Write the spelling word that matches each definition.

9. animals with wings _____

10. humans _____

11. animals related to dogs _____

12. plants that cover a lawn _____

Name _____ Date _____

Long oo and Short oo

choose	food	foolish	good
looked	rooster	took	wooden

Write a spelling word that goes with the other two words.

1. select, pick, _____

2. silly, ridiculous, _____

3. farm, chicken _____

4. observed, saw, _____

5. logs, timber, _____

6. excellent, great, _____

7. edible, nourishing, _____

8. removed, got hold of, _____

Write a spelling word to complete each sentence.

9. The _____ table is made from an oak tree.

10. There is so much _____ in the refrigerator.

11. I woke up to the sound of a _____ crowing.

12. She had to _____ between the ham sandwich

and the turkey sandwich.

Grammar, Spelling & Vocabulary Activity Book • © Benchmark Education Company, LLC   G3 U6 W2 BLM1

Name _____ Date _____

Long oo and Short oo

choose	food	foolish	good
looked	rooster	took	wooden

Write the correct spelling words.

Spelling words with short *oo*

1. _____   2. _____

3. _____   4. _____

Spelling words with long *oo*

5. _____   6. _____

7. _____   8. _____

Fill in the boxes for the spelling word *wooden*.

meaning	sentence
non-examples (wooden)	**sentence showing another meaning**

/ou/ as in how and out

brown	down	found	growls
howl	snout	sound	waterfowl

Write a spelling word that goes with the other two words.

1. black, gray, _____

2. discovered, recognized, _____

3. snarls, barks, _____

4. groan, moan, _____

5. nose, beak, _____

6. noise, tone, _____

7. below, under, _____

8. ducks, geese, _____

Circle the incorrect word in each sentence. Then write the spelling word that makes the sentence correct.

9. I'm so happy that I frond you! _____

10. Have you ever heard coyotes hole at night? _____

11. Stay away if the dog grills at you. _____

12. The grass is brain because we haven't had rain. _____

/ou/ as in how and out

brown	down	found	growls
howl	snout	sound	waterfowl

Write the spelling words for the given spelling pattern.

Spelling words with *ow*

1. _____ 2. _____

3. _____ 4. _____

5. _____

Spelling words with *ou*

6. _____ 7. _____

8. _____

Write the spelling word that is an antonym or a synonym of the bold word.

9. **lost** antonym: _____

10. **snarls** synonym: _____

11. **nose** synonym: _____

12. **up** antonym: _____

Suffixes -er, -or

actors	bakers	owners	painters
players	sculptors	vendors	visitors

Write the spelling word that matches each definition.

1. people whose works hang on museum walls _____

2. people who come to your home to see you _____

3. people who perform in plays and movies _____

4. the people to whom pets belong _____

5. people who carve objects out of clay _____

Circle the incorrect word in each sentence. Then write the spelling word that makes the sentence correct.

6. Those bankers make delicious pies and cakes. _____

7. Some venters at the market sell fruit, while others

sell vegetables. _____

8. Who are the planners on the baseball team? _____

9. We are expecting visors for dinner. _____

10. The anchors in that play were great! _____

Suffixes -er, -or

actors	bakers	owners	painters
players	sculptors	vendors	visitors

Write the spelling words for the given suffix.

Spelling words that end with _-er_

1. _____

2. _____

3. _____

4. _____

Spelling words that end with _-or_

5. _____

6. _____

7. _____

8. _____

Complete each definition with a spelling word.

9. _____ are people who perform.

10. People who make breads and cakes are _____.

11. _____ are people who come to see you.

12. People who have pets are the pets' _____.

Homophones

eight	so	wear	passed
past	ate	sew	where

Write a spelling word to complete each sentence.

1. It was raining, _____ the picnic was canceled.

2. Elena _____ pizza for lunch.

3. _____ is the lunchroom?

4. Please _____ the button on my coat.

5. My family has many traditions from _____

   generations that we still practice today.

Write the spelling word that best completes each analogy.

6. **Ball** is to **play** as **needle** is to _____.

7. **Say** is to **said** as **eat** is to _____.

8. **Six** is to **three** as _____ is to **four**.

9. **Apple** is to **eat** as **hat** is to _____.

10. **Kicked** is to **soccer** as _____ is to **football**.

Name _____ Date _____

Homophones

eight	so	wear	passed
past	ate	sew	where

Write the spelling words for the given number of letters.

Spelling words with 2 letters

1. _____

Spelling words with 3 letters

2. _____   3. _____

Spelling words with 4 letters

4. _____   5. _____

Spelling words with 5 letters

6. _____   7. _____

Spelling word with 6 letters

8. _____

Write the spelling word that matches each clue.

9. consumed food _____

10. the total number of shoes in four pairs _____

11. opposite of the present _____

12. fix with a needle and thread _____

Variant Vowel /ô/

awful	called	dawn	pause
stalks	taught	thawing	walls

Write the spelling word that best completes each analogy.

1. **Night** is to **morning** as **dusk** is to _____.

2. **Good** is to **great** as **bad** is to _____.

3. **Flowers** are to **blossoms** as _____ are to **stems**.

4. **Melting** is to _____ as **icy** is to **frozen**.

5. **Windows** are to _____ as **skylights** are to **ceilings**.

6. _____ is to **instructed** as **stopped** is to **paused**.

Fill in the boxes for the spelling word *pause*.

meaning	sentence
synonym	**homophone**
antonym	

(pause)

Variant Vowel /ô/

awful	called	dawn	pause
stalks	taught	thawing	walls

Write the spelling words for the given spelling pattern.

Spelling words with _al_

1. _____   2. _____

3. _____

Spelling words with _aw_

4. _____   5. _____

6. _____

Spelling words with _au_

7. _____   8. _____

Write the spelling word that is an antonym or a synonym of the bold word.

9. **continue**   antonym: _____

10. **stems**   synonym: _____

11. **instructed**   synonym: _____

12. **wonderful**   antonym: _____

Hard c and Soft c

affect	certain	computers	Connecticut
covered	crucial	fierce	recommended

Write the spelling word that matches each clue.

1. vital, important _____

2. aggressive, intense _____

3. a state in New England _____

4. having something on top _____

5. influence _____

Circle the incorrect word in each sentence. Then write the spelling word that makes the sentence correct.

6. My friend represented some new books to me. _____

7. I like only curtain types of snacks. _____

8. We looked up the answer on the commuters. _____

9. I still needed crystal pieces of information to solve the mystery.

_____

10. I am going to visit my cousin in connectors. _____

 Grammar, Spelling & Vocabulary Activity Book • © Benchmark Education Company, LLC

Hard c and Soft c

affect	certain	computers	Connecticut
covered	crucial	fierce	recommended

Write the correct spelling words.

Spelling words with the hard *c* sound

1. _____   2. _____

3. _____   4. _____

5. _____

Spelling words with the soft *c* sound

6. _____

7. _____

Spelling word with both the hard *c* and the soft *c* sounds

8. _____

Complete each sentence by writing a spelling word.

9. Hartford is the capital city of _____.

10. I was cold, so I _____ my legs with a blanket.

11. What was that movie you _____ to me the other day?

12. The invention of _____ changed the world.

Hard g and Soft g

again	garden	generous	green
grateful	germinated	gathered	good

Write the spelling word for each clue.

1. Growing from a seed _____

2. The color of grass _____

3. Being better than average _____

4. Happening multiple times _____

5. Things brought together _____

6. Giving a lot _____

7. Patch of land with flowers or vegetables _____

8. Feeling thankful _____

Write the spelling word that completes each analogy.

9. Better is to **worse** as _____ is to **bad**.

10. Flower is to _____ as **tree** is to **forest**.

Name _____ Date _____

Hard g and Soft g

| again | garden | generous | green |
| grateful | germinated | gathered | good |

Write the correct spelling words.

Spelling words with the hard _g_ sound

1. _____   2. _____

3. _____   4. _____

5. _____   6. _____

Spelling words with the soft _g_ sound

7. _____   8. _____

Write the spelling word that is an antonym or a synonym of the bold word.

9. **repeatedly**   synonym: _____

10. **greedy**   antonym: _____

11. **thankless**   antonym: _____

12. **assembled**   synonym: _____

Diphthongs

cloud	downpour	moisture	point
showers	soil	south	sprout

Write the spelling word that goes with the other two words.

1. overcast, nimbus,

_____

2. wet, damp,

_____

3. storm, raining,

_____

4. seed, plant,

_____

5. north, west,

_____

6. dirt, mud,

_____

7. spot, location,

_____

8. rainy, stormy,

_____

Fill in the boxes for the spelling word *showers*.

meaning	sentence
synonyms ⬭ showers	**sentence showing another meaning**

Diphthongs

cloud	downpour	moisture	point
shower	soil	south	sprout

Write the correct spelling words for each spelling pattern.

Spelling words with *ou*

1. _____   2. _____

3. _____   4. _____

Spelling words with *oi*

5. _____   6. _____

7. _____

Spelling words with *ow*

8. _____   9. _____

Write a spelling word to complete each sentence.

10. A tree's roots extend beneath the _____.

11. During the _____, the car's windshield wipers were moving at full speed.

12. As I stood in the greenhouse, I could feel the _____ in the air.

Suffixes -less, -ful, -able

countless	delightful	fanciful	penniless
profitable	sizeable	tearful	valuable

Write a spelling word that goes with the other two words.

1. endless, infinite,

_____

2. poor, broke,

_____

3. worthwhile, fruitful,

_____

4. amusing, enjoyable,

_____

5. sad, sobbing,

_____

6. gigantic, enormous,

_____

7. imaginative, whimsical,

_____

8. treasured, prized,

_____

Fill in the boxes for the spelling word *valuable.*

meaning	sentence
examples	**related words**
	antonym:
	synonym:

valuable

Suffixes -less, -ful, -able

countless	delightful	fanciful	penniless
profitable	sizeable	tearful	valuable

Write the correct spelling words for the given suffix.

Spelling words that end with *-less*

1. _____   2. _____

Spelling words that end with *-able*

3. _____   4. _____

5. _____

Spelling words that end with *-ful*

6. _____   7. _____

8. _____

Write a spelling word to complete each sentence.

9. _____ raindrops fall from the sky during a rain shower.

10. Our school bake sale made a _____ amount of money.

11. The sale was more _____ than we expected.

12. I got _____ at the end of the movie.

Prefixes dis-, un-

disappeared	disassembled	disbelief	displeasure
unblemished	unhappy	unrivaled	unsalted

Write the spelling word that matches each definition.

1. took apart

_____

2. the opposite of joy

_____

3. dropped out of sight

_____

4. flawless, not damaged

_____

5. excellent, without compare

_____

6. bland, tasteless

_____

7. sad, forlorn

_____

8. refusal to accept as true

_____

Circle the incorrect word in each sentence. Then write the spelling word that makes the sentence correct.

9. Our football team hasn't lost a game. We are unraveled.

_____

10. My cat has disapproved. Can you help me find her?

_____

11. Some people prefer their food to be unusable.

_____

12. The bike has been disabled, so we have to put it back together.

_____

Prefixes dis-, un-

disappeared	disassembled	disbelief	displeasure
unblemished	unhappy	unrivaled	unsalted

Write the correct spelling words for the given prefix.

Spelling words that begin with the prefix *dis-*

1. _____   2. _____

3. _____   4. _____

Spelling words that begin with *un-*

5. _____   6. _____

7. _____   8. _____

Write the spelling word that is an antonym or a synonym of the bold word.

9. **joyous**   antonym: _____

10. **flawless**   synonym: _____

11. **evaporated**   synonym: _____

12. **comparable**   antonym: _____

Prefixes pre-, re-

prearrange	prekindergarten	preorder	prepackaged
reconsider	recycled	restock	rethink

Write the spelling word that matches each definition.

1. used again for a purpose

_____

2. consider again

_____

3. plan ahead of time

_____

4. nursery school

_____

5. get new supplies

_____

6. wrapped before sale

_____

7. buy before it is for sale

_____

8. change your mind

_____

Fill in the boxes for the spelling word *recycle.*

meaning	sentence
things that get recycled	**related words** synonym: antonym:

(recycle)

Prefixes pre-, re-

prearrange	prekindergarten	preorder	prepackaged
reconsider	recycled	restock	rethink

Write the spelling words for the given prefix.

Spelling words that begin with *re-*

1. _____   2. _____

3. _____   4. _____

Spelling words that begin with *pre-*

5. _____   6. _____

7. _____   8. _____

Write a spelling word to complete each sentence.

9. The committee decided to _____

   Pam's application.

10. I decided to _____ my essay topic.

11. This bin is made out of _____ plastic.

12. The grocery store sells _____ fruits and

    vegetables.

Compound Words

bone-tired	daybreak	everyone	finish line
halfway	jack-rabbit	meanwhile	slow-poke

Write a spelling word for each clue.

1. extremely exhausted and worn out _____

2. extremely sluggish _____

3. all the people in a group _____

4. where a race ends _____

5. when an event is happening at the same time as another

event _____

6. a type of hare that is very quick _____

7. when the sun appears in the morning _____

8. the place equally distant from the beginning and the

end _____

Write the spelling word that completes each analogy.

9. Before is to **after** as **starting line** is to _____.

10. Exhausted is to _____ as **energetic** is to **lively**.

Compound Words

bone-tired	daybreak	everyone	finish line
halfway	jack-rabbit	meanwhile	slow-poke

Write the spelling words that use a hyphen.

1. _____

2. _____

3. _____

Write the spelling words that do not use a hyphen.

4. _____

5. _____

6. _____

7. _____

8. _____

Complete each sentence by writing a spelling word.

9. _____ comes after nighttime.

10. I was so close to the end of the race that I could see the

_____.

11. I wanted to get to school early but my brother was being a

_____.

12. I was happy when I found out I knew _____

at the party.

Suffixes -ing, -ness, -ment

amazement	cleverness	contentment	happiness	leading
sadness	scrambling	slyness	warning	

Write the spelling word that completes each sentence.

1. I looked at the incredible, giant statue in _____.

2. The relaxing music gave me a feeling of _____.

3. I jumped up and down in _____ when we won the championship!

4. We decided to pay attention to the _____ and not go in the cave.

5. The hike was too tough and we ended up _____ on the rocks!

Fill in the boxes for the spelling word _sadness_.

meaning	sentence
antonyms	**related words**
	root:
	adverb:
	synonym:

sadness

Suffixes -ing, -ness, -ment

amazement	cleverness	contentment	happiness	leading
sadness	scrambling	slyness	warning	

Write the spelling words for the given suffix.

Spelling words that end with *-ment*

1. _____   2. _____

Spelling words that end with *-ness*

3. _____   4. _____

5. _____   6. _____

Spelling words that end with *-ing*

7. _____   8. _____

9. _____

Write the spelling word that matches each definition.

10. quick thinking _____

11. stealth _____

12. tell to be careful _____

13. joy _____

Related Words

inventor	invention	problem	problematic
solution	solve	transformation	transforms

Write the spelling word that completes each analogy.

1. Creator is to **creation** as **inventor** is to _____.

2. Talk is to **speak** as **changes** is to _____.

3. Fix is to **broken** as _____ is to **problem**.

4. Easy is to _____ as **light** is to **dark**.

5. Answer is to _____ as **sad** is to **miserable**.

Fill in the boxes for the spelling word *transformation*.

meaning	sentence
something that transforms	related words
	verb:
	antonym:
	synonym:

(transformation)

Related Words

inventor	invention	problem	problematic
solution	solve	transformation	transforms

Write the spelling words for the given number of syllables.

Spelling words with 1 syllable

1. _____

Spelling words with 2 syllables

2. _____   3. _____

Spelling words with 3 syllables

4. _____   5. _____

6. _____

Spelling words with 4 syllables

7. _____   8. _____

Write the spelling word that is an antonym or a synonym of the bold word.

9. **problem**   antonym: _____

10. **creation**   synonym: _____

11. **changes**   synonym: _____

12. **imitator**   antonym: _____